SEVENTH

ANNIVERSARY ADDRESS

BEFORE THE

Platonian Literary Society

OF

M'KENDREE COLLEGE,

BY

PROF. J. B. TURNER,

APRIL 21, 1856.

"VIA SAPIENTIÆ."

PRINTED AT THE LITERARY GEM OFFICE, LEBANON, ILL.

CORRESPONDENCE.

PLATO HALL, 22d April, 1856.

PROF. J. B. TURNER:—

By the unanimous vote of the members of the Platonian Literary Society, I am instructed to request that you will place at their disposal, a copy of the highly interesting Address delivered before them on last evening.

With profound respect,

Yours,

D. S. KENNEDY, *Cor. Sec.*

MR. D. S. KENNEDY:

Corresponding Sec'y of Platonian Society of M'Kendree College,

DEAR SIR—Entertaining the sentiments which I do, it could not be otherwise than that I should be highly pleased with the favorable opinion your Society have expressed respecting the discourse alluded to; and as I have not time to review and correct, I submit it to your disposal, as delivered.

Yours truly,

J. B. TURNER.

JACKSONVILLE, May 1st, '56.

ADDRESS.

DIOGENES' CANDLE, OR THE SEARCH FOR TRUE MANHOOD.

My Friends, the theme I have selected for the present occasion, is somewhat uniqe, both in its aim and in its name. It is a theme of great interest, and of great practical importance at all times.

I shall aim at nothing new, but only to give utterance to the thought that already lies deeply *hidden* in the heart and soul of every one of my hearers. If I speak truthfully, you will therefore recognize the fact; and you will also perceive that Jesus Christ taught, lived, and acted out, essentially, the same truths, long before we were born. For he ALONE is the way, the truth, the life and the light of man. But if I so speak, I shall not speak in accordance with any mode of human opinion, or usuage, or form that ever yet existed on earth. For true Christianity never was, or will be organized or expressed in any authoritative human creed or form, until men are far wiser and purer than even the best of us now are.

You all remember the story of the old cynic Philosopher, *Diogenes*, who on being asked the reason why he lit a candle at noon-day, replied—"*Anthropon Zeto*"—"I seek a MAN." If we throw ourselves back to the time of that Philosopher, some two or three centuries before Christ, and contemplate the manners and the morals of *that* age, we must admit that there was both appositeness and truth in his act and his reply. If we were to maintain, however, that there is the same need of that candle now, or, in other words, that the world has made no *real, substantial* advance in the two thousand years past, we should be more cynical than the cynic himself. But still it may not be unprofitable, even for us to *take that candle in hand* and truly ascertain where we *do* and where we *do not* find a MAN. In order to do this, we will inquire

1st. What is True Manhood?

2d. Where is it found, and how produced?

WHAT THEN, IS TRUE MANHOOD?

Plato's definition, that "a man is a two-legged animal, without feathers," may answer as a general description; but the old philosopher who plucked the feathers from a dead rooster and threw it upon the table, exclaiming, "there is Plato's man," has shown us we need something more definite.

What, then, is True Manhood?

The essentials of true manhood do not relate to form, color, or size.—They are not qualities to be measured by the yard, or sold by the pound. They rise infinitely above, not only all physical, but also all mere intellectual attributes

We do not prize even the horse, mainly for his harness, nor yet for his strength, beauty, or speed. There is something even in this brute animal, behind and above all this, which we prize infinitely more than all these qualities together, when existing alone. He has strength and speed. But how does he use them, to serve or to kill his master? *That is the question*, and the main question. How much more, then, in man? He has wealth, capacity, talents, power, but *how does he use them?* That is the question

"Were I so tall to reach the pole,
And grasp the ocean in my span,
I must be meausured by my soul,
For 'tis the *soul* that makes the man."

And he may have all desirable qualities of birth, fortune, wealth, rank, title, talent, learning, language, science, genius and skill—and still, in the true, popular sense of the term, *no soul*—not one particle of true manhood; while on the other hand, he may be without any one, or even all of these, and still possess the very highest attributes of which humanity is capable.

THE MORAL QUALITIES in all subjects, capable of even a semblance of moral action, are infinitely higher, more valuable and more praiseworthy than any or all others combined. *Trustworthiness* is the very highest attribute of all beings created and uncreated; and we deceive ourselves if we imagine that *in the deep secret of our souls*, we do not ourselves so esteem it. But there are so many occasions in the ordinary intercourse of life, in which we are said to *trust* our fellow men, where no such thing really occurs, that it may, at first sight, seem otherwise. For example:—We entrust our property or money, or even our lives, in the hands of men whom we know are utterly selfish, unprincipled, and corrupt at heart; but we also know that the man is rich, the note is signed, the bond is sealed, and the LAW is STRONG. The thing we really confide in, in all such cases, is the money, the bond and the law, and not in the man at all. This low, but common example, will serve to illustrate the priciple in other and higher relations.

What, then, are the vital elements of this trustworthiness?

I answer. They are all essentially *moral* and *heroic* in their nature, the fundamental elements of all *true manhood*, and all *real* virtue. They are these: Courage, Magnanimity, Generosity, Fidelity. Courage, as opposed to cowardice or timidity; magnanimity, as opposed to meanness; generosity, as opposed to selfishness; fidelity, as opposed to treachery. Without these there can be no *trustworthiness*, no *true manhood* and no *real virtue*, though man had an angel's intellect, a seraph's beauty, or a satan's power.

The essence of all these qualities concentrated, are expressed in the thirteenth chapter of Corinthians, by the Greek word "*agape*"—*Benevolence*. They have become perfectly incarnate and perfectly exemplified on earth only in one person—the DIVINE MAN, OUR LORD AND SAVIOR, JESUS CHRIST.

Some may, perhaps, feel no little surprise that Courage should be placed as a first attribute in this category. Napoleon, say they, was courageous, but Jesus was humble. I will not pause to quarrel with the shallow gibberish of theologies and ecclesiastics on this point. God knows they have reason enough for ruling all true manhood out of Christianity, if they themselves are to stand before the world as specimens of it. But in my opinion, it required more true courage to live the life that Jesus did, for a single week, than it has to fight all the battles ever fought since the ark swam on the waters of the flood. And in this opinion, I think the most intelligent and devout of our American religious teachers will agree with me. But if any man thinks otherwise, let him try it; then he will know for himself.

Among ancient Worthies who gave to the world the most illustrious proofs of this *true manhood*, we might mention Abraham and Joseph among the patriarchs; Moses, the law-giver; David, and Daniel, and Isaiah; Paul, the apostle, and John the beloved disciple.

Among the great cloud of modern witnesses, I find no other so full and perfect example as that of our immortal WASHINGTON. And if we should seek it in the humbler walks of life, and not find a living specimen near us, we might take the fanciful delineation of the far-famed "Uncle Tom," whose equal, either in the high or low degrees of real life, we shall never find. But as my object is simply to illustrate, it will subserve my present purpose well. From all of which the obvious corallery will be self evident—that the true Disciple, or follower, or imitator of Christ will have true manhood, true trustworthiness, courage, generosity, magnanimity and fidelity—*true virtue.*

True WOMANHOOD consists, of course, in the very self-same qualities in the opposite sex; and there can be no true womanhood without them, however much of music and Millinery, French and "flosofee," Latin and logic, of polish and posies, of airs and antics there may be. I shall use the term Manhood, therefore, for the sake of brevity, to designate these same qualities in either sex.

It is easy to train a tiger or a donkey,
To make a manakin or a monkey.

To raise a parrot, a mocking bird, a whippoorwill or a peacock, but to make a *man* or a *woman* is hard—the very noblest work of Almighty God.

It is well for us to notice, in passing, that these high qualities, when they exist, ALWAYS produce their necessary and legitimate effects of *thorough and radical reform.* It was so in our Savior's time, in Martin Luther's time, in the stirring times of the Commonwealth, and the American Revolution. It is even so in the sons of truly illustrious and noble mothers. "By their fruits ye shall know them." And where their fruits *are not,* they *are not,* though the whole world may be filled with their professions, their semblances, and their shams.

Look, for example, at the French people, ever amid the uproar and glare of war, carnage and revolution; yet in reality the most detestably mean and cowardly civilized nation on earth. And their "nationale glaire" (as I believe they very properly, almost spell and pronounce it,) is only the necessary consequence of that detestable cowardice and meanness of their people, which enables one daring villain to gather them all together, and drive them before him for any purpose of blood or perfidy, now for the Republic, now for the Empire, and now for nothing, like a flock of senseless geese or sheep. If there is any true courage, or real glory or manhood in such a national character as that, may the Lord deliver us from it. A brawling cut-throat or bully, is always, at heart, a most arrant coward; and the same is true of nations as of individuals. Noble exceptions, it is true, we find. Lafayette, companion and friend of Washington; Napoleon, prince of heroes in war, and had he found a people worthy of such matchless endowments, none can tell what he might have been. But it is well to glance at the *value* and *power* of this true manhood.

All things in this world are on sale. Everything has its fixed value. But the price of this Manhood is very high, for it is very valuable. Gold or goods can buy other things, but nothing but eternal right and truth can purchase this. He that would buy it or command it to his service, must have the infinite treasure of Heaven, and the resources of God to proffer as its reward. It is no family patrimony or heir-loom, descending from father to son, as the heritage of original sin is bequeathed in the catechisms, from Adam to all his posterity, or as the divine right descends through long lines of successful usurpers. It can neither be ennobled by ancestry or patrimony, nor degraded by poverty. Rank can give it no dignity. Conquests, triumphs and ovations cannot exalt it, nor can overthrow, defeat and disaster, however great, either despoil or degrade it. It asks, and it can receive no glory, no dignity or worth not already its own. Power, rank, wealth, intellect, fame, may indeed serve it, but they can neither enrich or exalt it. It is the same in all the essentials of its true glory, whether in purple or in rags; in prison or in paradise; on the cross or on the *throne*. It gives a light to all it touches. It gives, but it borrows none. A *real* character, like the fabulous one of Uncle Tom, for example, would exert a more lasting and renowned influence on the destiny of these United States, under whatever seeming disadvantages, than all the mere office-seekers and office-holders, from the President downwards, that ever trod the continent, with all their prestige of rank and power, and their outward means of influence and fame; and I am not sure but the bare imaginary conception of such a character will do it.

Jesus Christ, by the simple, natural force of this true manhood manifested in him, independently of all considerations of his divine power—without rank or office; without learning a book or writing a letter, has, in fact, exerted a deeper and more lasting influence on the human race, than all the emperors, warriors, statesmen, philosophers, poets and divines, that have ruled, and fought, and struggled, and taught, and sung, and preached from Adam's day to our own.

If mere knowledge is power; if eloquence and logic; if armies and navies that go and come at their bidding, are powerful, true Manhood is *omnipotent*, for it wields the infinite resources of God. Compared with this, all the resources and instruments of good; all the little arts of strategy and diplomacy; all the little expediencies of little souls in little power, whether of arts or of arms, of eloquence, or of song—they are all, *all* little, inefficient, weak and contemptible in their achievments as well as in their methods and ends.

If in symbol we should compare the animal and physical powers of man, their strength and perfection and beauty of form, to the green and gladsome earth, ever varient in its lights and shadows, and his intellectual powers to the radient glory of the sun, imparting light and life to all, we must still say that these higher moral endowments are the very pavilion of the Almighty itself, whence all this subordinate light and life and beauty and glory and harmony proceed.

We all admit the abstract power of truth. We all know the beautiful lines,

> "Truth, struck to earth shall rise again;
> The eternal years of God are hers;
> But Error, wounded, writhes in pain,
> And dies amid her worshippers."

This truth, when uttered to the winds by the babbling child, when impressed with printer's ink (mere lampblack and oil) on cotton paper, is still *immortal*. When adorned by the genius of poetry and eloquence, it is *potent* and inspired, and wields the powers, the armies and destinies of earth. But when *incarnate*, living, acting, and breathing forth its divine spirit in the highest and most illustrious forms of true virtue and real Manhood, it is not only potent and immortal, but Omnipotent and Divine, and wields the destinies, not of earth alone, but of eternal years and worlds to come.

When pure and unmingled with all human selfishness and sin, it *was God manifested in the flesh*; its power was the power of God; and its triumphs and its destiny were the triumphs and the destiny of Heaven and of God forever more—fit, and alone fit to have a name given it above every name, and to be exalted above all thrones, principalities, dominions and powers, in Heaven above and on earth beneath.

Bring forth, now, all the gibes and sophistries and witticisms, and sneers of hoary and consecrated falsehood and vice; all the little expediences of race and tribe; all the miserable quibbles of sect and school; invoke the genious of your philosophers, and the inspiration of your eloquence and song; appeal to the magic of your wealth and your art; call upon the memory of the renowned dead, and summon the illustrious living around you; marshal them in the full strength of their empires and their armies, and with all the pride and power of their navies, and bid them *crush the wretch* which your own demon soul can alone see in that *incarnate truth*. How vain! That true Manhood—that incarnate Truth is more invincible than all the arts and powers of earth and hell. Though in rags; though beggard and begging; though in the dungeon, or stretched upon the rack, or swinging upon the gibbet or the cross—its very dungeon shall be all radient with the light of Heaven; around its cross the solid earth shall quake; the sun shall hide itself in darkness, and the moon in blood; and the very agony of its groans shall fall on the ears of the coming generations like the music of the spheres. It shall hush, in a silence that may be felt, the tongue of all other eloquence and all other song. Your philosophies shall be abashed and confounded at its presence; the illustrious dead shall all be forgotten, and the millions of the living shall stand still before God. The power of wealth shall cease to charm. Your embattled hosts shall stand aghast; and the sword and the spear of the warrior shall enter his own soul. But God's INCARNATE TRUTH shall live and triumph over all.

True Manhood HAS a power on earth which nothing else save the true Divinity has; and in human sympathy and regard, it rivals even that.

Now, let it here be distinctly noted and admitted that we have an abundant supply of *dead truth* in all our Constitutions, declarations and parchment manifestations; in all our sermons, expostulations, ejaculations, and (in all conscience) it is usually dead enough, though even it is destined to a future resurrection of immortality and life; but there is more real power in one living, breathing Washington or Kossuth, than there would be in all the paper declarations and constitutions that could be written on the whole continent, if it were all but one tanned sheepskin, and more real efficiency in one truly martyr man or woman, though a beggar, than there can be in all the sermons and prayers and services that could be repeated from one Christmas night to another, the world around, without any such manifestation.

With the one, with great parades of logic and eloquence, and great bladders full of windy patriotism, great agonies of exhortation and expostulation in great churches full of little vanities, we may, at least, seem to keep ourselves and our fellows in society, where we are, like drowning men clinging to a dead log or an old hulk; but when God sends along that *steamship*, a true, living Man, how easily we are borne forward and delivered at once from our agonisms and our perils!

May Heaven's mercy send us *a Man*. All this little fillibustering around old figments and old forms don't seem to do. Loud thumps on the old hulk don't seem to make us swim any faster. We want a new craft with new engineering and new speed. The old hulk did well enough once. It was, indeed, a fine and a most gallant ship. She crossed the gulf of the Dark Ages, and she stemmed the storms of the Revolution like a swan in an angry sea. But with *our own hands* we have torn away the masts and the sails, ripped up the decks, and thrown away the compass and the rudder, because a few old grannies on board told us it was "expedient," and we wanted to "compromise" and "keep peace" with the STORM and the WIND. Now, we need a new ship. God send us a new *Martyr-Man*, to construct it for us, or at least, to refit and RE-MAN the old one.

We have had many great and illustrious tinkers on board; great champions of little figments. *Search them with your candle*, and you will find them, though vauntingly great, infinitely small. *What have they done*, that was not better done before they were born, or likely to die before they are dead? After all our rhapsodies and eulogies and rhodomantades, when or where have we seen a truly great man since we buried the Patriot Fathers? And even on the small scale, does any man in his senses believe, that with all our schools and means and churches and wealth, there is, at this moment, as much True Manhood and True Womanhood among the twenty millions of the present generation, as there was among the three millions of the Revolution? I confess I do not. There are many who doubt it. May Heaven in its mercy send us a Man.

1st. But it must be confessed that this true Manhood, in its *higher manifestations*, is not the product of every age and clime. Nor can it be expected to be. It is in this degree, only the slow growth of the toiling ages; that, like angel's visits, are few and far between.

But in its lower degrees it is ever with us; for God always reserves a seed on earth to secure him. The salt of the earth is never taken fully away, though its moral and political SAVIORS, we have not always with us.

2d. Where, then, shall we find these lower manifestations of true manhood? I answer, it is not the exclusive product of any particular race, rank, cast, creed, profession, or pursuit in life. If you survey human society, like the several champions of tribe or sect, or like the Fourth of July orator, as the owl at noon-day surveys from the masthead the vast and dazzling deep around him, you will find it, of course, all in one race, or tribe, or clan.

The Anglo-Saxon beholds its evidences only in his Magna Chartas, his protestant and political professions and manifestoes; his prodigies of Art and of Power; his open bibles, churches, and polls, and his free schools and colleges; open and free, of course, to all who are allowed to enjoy them (just as they are in Italy and Russia,) AND TO NO OTHERS.

The Catholic of Europe sees it in his holy Mother Church, with its erudite priesthood, its gorgeous ritual and venerated altars, free, alike, to all colors, classes, climes and ages; in the ancient and divine right of reigning kings, rather than in the modern right of apostate Republicans—a *bible* honestly open and duly submissive to the priesthood, and *honestly* shut to all others. He deplores the apostacy and treason of our Luthers and of our Washingtons, and realizes the extreme depravity of such rebels and miscreants as Mazzini and Kossuth; and duly curses and anathematises the horrid barbarism and detestable hypocrisy of our agrarian, infidel, slave-holding Democracy, as he is pleased to term it.

The Mormon in his Salt Lake home, finds, *there alone*, the pure, patriarchal faith of the elder and the younger Joseph. The Gentile world all without, fit plunder for the faithful few; and even the Camanche chief, as he bears to his wigwam the scalps of pioneer adventurers, exults in the greatness of his triumphs, the justice of his cause, and the glory of his race and power.

So it was in the olden time, with Jews, Greeks, and Romans; and so it is in every age. The *true Manhood*, in their estimation, is ever all inside of that WOODEN HORSE of policy or of faith which their own vanity, pride, or perfidy has constructed and consecrated to the gods, as at once a defence to themselves and a perfidious engine of destruction to their followers.

Take your candle into the belly of that wooden horse; search it closely; you will find the perfidious *Greek*, and not the true man there. Carry it through all the outward forms and organizations that have ever existed upon earth, and you will find no monopoly of real virtue or real vice in any one of them. But one great, wondrous miracle running through them all, *Human Nature*, marvelously the same; marvelously alike under all climes, races, names, forms, and ages, and the *divine nature, true manhood*, rarely found among them all.

I am aware that this view of things is not very consoling to our Protestant, Anglo-Saxon vanity; but it cannot be helped, till we reform in deed and in truth, as well as in profession and pretense.

Leaving, then, these general surveys, let us descend, for a moment, with our candle, amid the ordinary pursuits of individual life, and examine the relative claims of *rank, profession*, and *pursuit;* and what shall we find? There stands one, gifted with the highest official rank which the acclaiming voices and votes of millions could confer. He has wealth, talent, education, power, all he ever desired—far more than he ever expected, is his. *Is he a Man?* Bring that candle, and search and see. You will find that necessity or accident, not virtue or merit, placed him where he is. He is not there because he had true manhood, but precisely because it was well known that he had not. A fit tool for dirty work was wanted, and in him it was found. They did not want a man, or, if they had, they could not have found one for such service. They wanted a two-legged animal, without feathers, for certain dirty uses, and there, aloft, he sits. Take your candle and examine him at your leisure; or rather, blow it out; he is not worth looking at.

In ordinary life, you shall find among merchants, mechanics, and farmers —men, skilled in all the varied arts of their calling, and blessed with the ample results of their skill, and still, if you examine them with your candle, you shall find nothing but the mere merchant, mechanic, or farmer—a mere tool, of no use to himself or any one else, except to transfer so many goods, like a locomotive, or erect so many structures, like a steam factory, or elaborate so many crops and products like the animals and tools he uses. A curious and a wonderful machine, indeed, but never, for once, put to any of the higher uses and ends for which its Maker designed it. No true manhood there—not a particle.

In all, the so called, learned professions, you will meet with precisely similar results. You shall find professors and teachers versed in all lore, ancient and modern; skilled in all science and all tongues. *Doctors of medicine* who have pills and powders and enigmatical prescriptions, and wondrous wise looks and saws, enough to kill or cure a whole generation of patients at a single dose. *Doctors of Law*, with all possible "ifs and ands," hems and haws, briefs, budgets, pleas and plaintiffs, expediences, quirks and quibbles, writs, rights and wrongs. Gabriel condemned and sentenced one hour, and Satan exalted and crowned the next, all by the potent force of immaculate justice, eloquence and law. Doctors of Divinity, full of all Greek and Hebrew, and all possible sectarian lore, with all possible exhortations, of all possible eloquence and power; cures for all sins, mortal and immortal, with sermons, prayers, hymns, psalms, absolutions and regenerations, orthodox, all old and tried, or in the newest style and warranted good. All these things, and many more, you shall find with your candle, in precise accordance with some dozen scores of different schools in law, medicine and divinity; and each antagonism warranted infallible by them all, in such admirable profusion and confusion, that every man, sick or well, innocent or guilty, saint or sinner, orthodox or hetrodox, may, at any time, touch and take, and take to his liking, be it good or bad.

But when you come to call for the MANHOOD of the administrator, you *may* find it not at home, or otherwise engaged; at any rate, it is not at your service, nor any one's else.

The truth is that human society needs, in its merely worldly and selfish workings, an annual production of so many eatables; so much beef, corn and pork; the manufacture of so many sweetmeats and nicknacks; the transfer and delivery of so much money and merchandize; the exhibit and defence of so many writs and pleas on the accidents and crimes of the process. Pills and powders to physic off the surfeit of consumption, or remove inevitable inflictions; and prayers and psalms and sermons enough to keep the conscience quiet in the great machine as it whirls and spins, *without agitation*, that is, without any practical interference with its whirling and spinning. And any man may engage in any one or all of these pursuits, and IN ONE JUST AS WELL AS ANOTHER, perform its requisite tread-mill round, with all imaginable grace and perfection, without, for once calling into action a single principle of his MORAL NATURE above those instincts of self-interest and self-preservation with which the brutes are in some degree endued. Large professions, spacious semblances, broad phylacteries, and glowing eulogies, it is true, everywhere abound; but do you *in all cases*, find *with your candle*, the corresponding reality? But *be it remembered*, you do find it in some cases, not a few. You *do find* the merchants, mechanics, farmers and divines, who *manfully, magnanimously, gloriously* fill their spheres, ply their skill, increase their comforts, heal the bodies, brighten the virtues, defend the rights and bless and save the souls of their fellow-men. All honor, then, to these faithful ones, be they few or many. Search then with your candle; they are worth looking at a long, long time.

But that our scrutiny may be severe, and that we may not be deceived in this search, we should ever remember that civilized, and especially, professedly christianized nations, carry their *real* sins through the world, not openly and boidly, like the savage, but covertly and under false labels, as the sot transports his drams under the Maine-liquor law, jostling the policeman as he goes. "What have you got there?" exclaims the man of the customs. "Oh, nothing but broadcloth, nothing but broadcloth, sir." Or, perhaps, "nothing but lath, tied lath, sir." But when the scrutanizing functionary begins to unrol the broadcloth, or untie the lath, out tumbles the "striped pig."

It is said that when the good people of the New Haven colony wanted to rob the Indians of their rich lands in Milford, they first called a church meeting and voted *unanimously*,

1st. That the earth is the Lord's, and the fulness thereof.

2d. The Lord hath given it to his saints.

3d. We are the saints of the Most High God, and these Indians are heathen and children of the devil.

Of course the Mormon inference soon followed and they took the land. Now, this fact or fable, as you please, illustrates our point. For these poor Indians would, probably, have entered upon any similar work without taking pains to wrap up their sins in scripture texts, with little care for the glory of God in the premises.

We call our wholesale robberies and murders, diplomacy and defence of national honor; and the very work which we begin and end with prayers and psalms, our more honest savage brother begins with the war-whoop, and ends with the war-dance. We advance with our chaplains and our psalters, he with only his tomahawk and his scalping-knife. But he is a savage, and has not yet learned to cut throats and rip bowels with all our pious care and skill.

Our detestable arrogance and pride we call propriety; our most dastardly meanness and servility we tie up in a nicely compacted bundle of lath, labelled *prudence*—firm bound on all sides and ready for show on all occasions. Our avarice, we men pack along through the world, under the name of industry, and providing for one's own household, while some of the other sex manage to carry along more devils with them than ever entered into Mary Magdalene, under the most admirable epithet of "*nervous*," "*very nervous indeed.*" How ungallant this is!! But that old candle of Diogenes will make us read things as they really are. Even our exhortations, our charities, and our very prayers are sometimes only the outer wrappers under which we the more deeply hide the vanity of our souls. But the striped pig is still there, and if there are any sins which we find it impossible thus to pack through the world, under the false labels of civilized life, unobserved of our fellows, our metaphysics and theologies readily furnish us with an ample supply of *substitutes, absolutions and equivalents, and theological figments and quibbles*; so that in our *estimate of things*, they neither wound our conscience, disturb our complacency, or mar or impair our virtue or our manhood.

But if we search human nature with our candle, we must of course, attend to all these things, and not condemn our savage brother because he carries his sins *openly*, by the natural handle, and excuse ourselves by hiding our own beneath those bundles of broad cloth nomenclature, and theological lath with which our nicer verbiage and more subtle dogmas have supplied us.

And surely, in view of all these counterfeits and delusions, we need, each of us, to search *our own selves* that we may truly know what manner of spirit we are of, and open our eyes and our hearts to all examples of *true manhood*, whenever and however found. If you search with your candle, you will find them. But if you look only with the owl-eyes of your race, your party or your sect, you never will.

"Say we not truly, thou art a Samaritan, and hast a devil, and art mad." "Not this man, but Barabbas." "Now Barabbas was a robber." Yet this was said of him who, alone, is holy and pure. In the narrow pass, at the battle of Lampach, Arnold Winklereid left the Swiss ranks, and rushing upon the Austrian spears, received as many as possible in his body, and thus broke through the line, and made way for liberty, as the poet says

"'Make way for liberty,' he cried,
Then ran with arms extended wide,
As if his *dearest friends* to clasp,
Ten spears he swept within his grasp;
He bowed among them like a tree,
And thus made way for liberty.
An earthquake could not overthrow,
A city with a surer blow,—
Thus Switzerland again was free,
Thus death *made way* for liberty."

Take now your candle; go forth into the wide world and search, and you shall find no age, or race, or class, bereft of all specimens of a similar illustrious virtue. They bring no credentials of college, school or class, but they come with the seal of the living God on their foreheads, and kings and empires bow before them.

Your shepherds, your fishermen and your tent-makers shall come forth from Judea, bearing greater blessings to the world than all her kings, councils, priests, Levites, synagogues and sanhedrims, through the whole thousands of years of their history. You shall find your Wickliffs, your Husses, your Luthers and Knoxes, who feared neither king, nor priest, nor pope; your Sidneys, who cared not for crowns nor commonwealths, in the same phalanx with your Washingtons, your Lafayettes, Kossuths and Mazzinis, leading onward to the great conflicts of the ages, the Armageddon's of earth's history, a whole host of swarthy martyrs and heroes nearer *to us*, but less known to fame. They shall come, despising the hollow mockery of your canonized faiths and the legalised villainies of your empires, your constitutions and your laws, proclaiming in the face of high Heaven, the *eternal justice of God*, the *rights of man*, and the *freedom of the soul*. They shall come with the sound of the trumpet and the voice of the archangel; and if you resist them, they shall dabble your bridle-reins in blood. Your crowned, voluptuous and besotted tyrants; your servile, feeling, sentimental priests shall tremble as they come; and your miserable, pettifogging demagogues, however gifted with talents, or exalted in office, shall fall before them. MAKE WAY FOR LIBERTY, for lo! they come. No profession or pursuit or class shall be unhonored. Your Cincinnati shall come forth from the plow; your Franklins from the printing office; your Shermans from the shoe-bench; your Bunyans from the tinker's shop; your learned blacksmiths from the anvil and the forge; your Touissaint L'Ouvertures, your Penningtons and Clarkes and Douglases, with skins all blackened with an African sun, but with the divine light of free and heaven-born souls, deemed on earth the slaves of your lusts, but counted in heaven with the masters of your doom, they shall come. Will you have the impudence to ask them for their pedigree? They shall answer you in the language of one of their own race, that their "ancestor was an ape, and that their lineage begins where yours ends."

In this embattled host of the present and the past, your Grecian Socrates, and your Roman Brutii, shall be marshalled with your Chinese Confucii and your Persian Zoroasters; your Catholic Fenelons, and Father Matthews, and your Lord Baltimores, with your Quaker Penns; your English Knoxes and American Roger Williamses and John Robinsons: your Emanuel Sweedenburgs; your Edwardses and your Dwights and Wesleys, with your Hancocks and Adamses; your skeptical Franklins and Jeffersons and Owens, and Blanco Whites; your invincible Logans and Osceolas; your swarthy Pocahontases and Powhattans, knowing *not God* but as they see him in the cloud or hear him in the wind, shall come forth from their dusky forest home, to *stay* the Christian Murder of your Placidoes and your martyr poet-slaves. All, all shall come to teach Christian Republicans the first truths of patriotism and freedom, and Christian schoolmen and polemics, the first lessons of love to God and man. If you are their oppressors, they shall gather your arrows and your spears to their bosoms; they shall turn their *faces* to your courts, your bayonets and your gibbets, but their *backs* to your altars, your nunneries and your prayers.

MAKE WAY FOR LIBERTY, FOR LO! THEY COME.—With souls of fire touched from the altar of God, like the cherubims in the prophet's vision, they shall move to meet you at their coming. "Their wings shall be joined in one; they shall not turn as they go." They shall go, every one straightforward. Whither the spirit leads them they shall go. And there shall be living wheels of fire that turn not, as they go; with clouds and whirlwinds and lightnings and thunderings and voices, and glowing coals of fire. And he that toucheth them shall die.

Plato's men—"two legged animals without feathers"—will stand a poor chance in this dread warfare, whether perched upon the sacred desk, or on the Senate's high and lofty tower. Marvel not, my hearer, that I put in this category of true and faithful manhood—faithful to God and man, some, who have not, indeed, been blessed with our outward means of light and knowledge. "For when the Gentiles, which have not the law, do by nature, the things contained in the law, these having not the law, are a law unto themselves. And shall not the uncircumcision which is by nature, if it keep the righteousness of the law, *judge thee* who by letter and circumcision, dost transgress the law? For he is not a Jew which is one outwardly; but he is a Jew who is one inwardly. Thou that preachest that a man should not steal; dost thou steal? Thou that abhorrest idols, dost thou commit sacrilige? Thou that makest thy boast in the law, through the breaking of the law, dishonorest thou God?"

So thought and so wrote the great apostle of the Gentiles; and I am not aware that the little figments and little fripperie of our modern theologists have, as yet, annihilated this great practical *revealed* truth.

Do you ask me how all these became children of the spirit? "The wind bloweth where it listeth, thou hearest the sound thereof, but canst not tell whence it cometh nor whither it goeth. So is *every one* that is borne of the spirit." But let us not imagine that our fair sisters of the other sex are either unrepresented or unhonored in this great procession of illustrious virtue and manhood.

To say nothing of the Ruths and Rachels and Esthers and Marys and Marthas and Dorcasses of olden time or of the Madame Guyenes, Hannah Mores, Lady Arabellas and Flora McDonalds; the Mrs. Washingtons, the Adamses, Williamses, Mottes, Elliotts and Caldwells of more recent days; when we see such specimens of womanhood abroad in the land, as we find in our own Miss Lyon, Mrs. Stowe, and the ever memorable and exalted Miss Dix, we are constrained to cry aloud and spare not: Ho, ye most honored and most honorables! Ye lords of all, most magnificent and profound!! Ye judges and senators most grave and noble!! Ye lawyers and philosophers most wise and prudent!! Ye divines most eloquent, learned and devout!! Ho ye! one and all. Now is the time for fear, for alarm, for terror, for caution, and for *action too*. For the nether garmets of your discarded manhood are fast slipping away from their appropriate sex. You have great and glorious leaders, *young ladies*. *Press on*, PRESS ON. And you, *young gentlemen*, take care of your small clothes, for you have rivals in the field far more dangerous than the Bloomerites.

Thus, while we search the world with our candle and discover its semblances, deceits and shams, in all ages and among all classes, professions and pursuits alike, we also find good men and true among them all, bearing the destinies of the race onward and upward, with united and resistless power, toward the jubilee of that great hour when all men shall be the free men of the Lord, and all the earth filled with the glory of his might.

3. *How then can we accelerate this great developement of character and of destiny*? I can answer only in brief:—It can be done only through the combined and co-operative educational influences of the FAMILY, the SCHOOL, the CHURCH and the STATE. Let it be shown in each and all of these, that *character—true manhood*—is really prized and sought, nurtured and honored; the thing really *wanted* and *aimed at*, instead of the mere varieties, mummeries and conformities of some local conventional *respectability* based on the outward glare of fashion, wealth, etiquette, dress, equippage, rank, office, learning, scholarship, intellect, eloquence, and all those nameless trifles which are now every where in the family and the church, as well as in the school and the state, placed before the great essentials of real character and true manhood. Let *this be seen and felt too*, not simply in these set harangues in which we attempt to deceive both ourselves and our children, (for we shall deceive neither,) but in our actual life, our social intercourse and daily conduct. Or, if we have not the manhood to do this, let us, at least, be consistent, and rule it out of our admonitions, our sermons and our prayers. As matters now are, the world is quite too full of pathetic, dandy-jack exhortations on the superlative value of virtue which our hearers and our children well know we do not believe one word of our-

selves, and should be quite provoked if we found them acting strictly according to our formal advice, *in any case*, except where it is already "*respectable*," that is, *fashionable* to do so.

"Have any of the Pharisees believed on him?" This is the first question the bond-slaves of "respectability ask in all ages. If *true manhood* is of more value than mere intellect or learning, or scholarship, or genius, or aught else under the sun, then let it be more fostered and cherished and cared for in our schools, seminaries and colleges, instead of less, or not at all. And let such courses of study and discipline alone be prescribed as shall tend most fully to develop and stregthen it; instead of such, as all experience shows, tend only to dwarf, cripple and emasculate it. If it is of more value to the state or church than all else, then let not the people of the State scout it from the polls, and drive it from every office in the land, or by other means, disfranchise and disown it; nor the church cast it out as an evil thing, because it discards her frivolities, or rebukes her follies or her sins.

"Thou art altogether born in sin, and dost thou teach us," said the bigotted Jews. "And they cast him out." Yet the LORD of ALL took him up. If in the family, the school, the church and the State alike—CHARACTER—TRUE MANHOOD—is to be the one great, sole end, ever in view; and if dress, manners, etiquette, customs, forms, ceremonies, sciences, literatures, scholarships, sermons, theologies, churches, offices, constitutions, and laws, one and ALL, are to be held and treated *not as ends*, but, as only the *humble means*, the mere instrumentalities to this ONE, SOLE, GREAT END—the nurture and developement, in all classes and races alike, of this *true manhood*; and if this whenever and wherever seen, is revered and prized more than *all else put together*; then, and not till then, the reign of Reason, of Truth, and of God shall come. Now if the family, the school and the church, really believe the honesthearted sincerity of this *true manhood* more valuable than the flippant deceits of etiquette, fashion and form; if they really prize its sun-burnt and toil-worn industry—at the plow—in the shop—in the kitchen and the washroom, more than the fantastic displays of a vicious and useless, self-indulgent idleness and ease—TRUE VIRTUE, in hovels and in rags—before pampered, voluptuous, effeminate vice in silks, satins and broadcloths;—if they really think its sober judgment, its manly thought, its earnest purpose, and its high resolves, for the *just*, the *right* and the *true*, of more account than the smirking displays of little, pedantic etiquettes, conformities and respectabilities at home and abroad,—if they really deem the *soul* greater than the *body*, and prize the man more than the monkey,—if *character* is to be placed *high above* all mere outward adornments or acquirements, whether of body or mind—*in one word*, if JESUS CHRIST is really to rule instead of Homer, or Horace, or Newton, or Euclid, or Mozart, or Beau Brummell—then let us act as if we believed it, and adjust our individual prejudices, our educational processes, our daily conversation and our laws of life and social intercourse to the views we profess; and we shall do more for the true millennium of God and of Christ in one week than we are likely to do now, by our eulogies and sermons and services in a whole century of sabbaths.

But do we do this? What is the real, practical standard of *acknowledged worth*, in the family, the social gathering, the church, the school and the state? Is it these great *moral elements* of all true virtue and manhood, or the dumb show and mummeries of our little conventional respectabilities? I do not ask which is put foremost in our lectures to our children—in our orations, sermons and prayers, but which is uppermost in our thoughts and hearts, and in all the practical and UNGUARDED manifestations of our real, inward life--week days and Sundays--at home and abroad--when we choose our representatives--hire our teachers or our preachers--visit our schools, our churches or our friends? Do all our religious professions and principles, for example, ever really touch or diminish our own pride of standing, profession or cast, any more than the religion of the Brahman of India does his? But if we allow our great Anglo Saxon god, *Respectability*, to perform precisely the same work in our souls and our social life, that the great god of Vishnoo performs in the soul and life of the Indian idolater, how are we better than he? If the sad work is inexorably done, what matters it by what name we choose to christen the imaginary idol that does it? Or, if *custom, respectability*, is to to be the real god of the soul, what matters it by what name it invokes it, in its formal devotion, whether of Vishnoo or Allah, or Jupiter, or Jehovah? Who does not feel at this moment that in the great Eastern struggle, the Ottoman worshippers of Allah are, in fact, more Christian than the pretended worshippers of Jehovah and Jesus, who are striving to rob and to crush them? God looketh upon the heart and trieth the reins of the children of men, and if the fact be wanting, the spacious pretensions can do no good.

Why should we despise our Chinese and Indian brethren who cripple their feet and tattoo their skins, while we cripple our lungs and tattoo our souls? Or why abjure our Hindoo brother who swings his body on the hock of eastern devotion, while we whirl our souls and the souls of our children around the same giddy circles of fashion and form?

"O, wad-some power the giftie gie us,
To see oursels as ithers see us!"

Again—while we continue to practice and emulate and extol the multiform *varieties* that demand the inevitable consumption of all our resources, why scourge and lash and curse the necessary avarice that feeds them? Do we not know that if one vice eats another must pay its bills?

My hearers, if we would again reproduce the true manhood and true womanhood of the apostolic or revolutionary times, we must adopt our means to our ends. We must *not* allow the great Anglo-Saxon god, *Respectability*, to perform precisely the same work in our souls and our society that the heathen god, Vishnoo, performs in the mind and casts of the Hindoo. We must *not* cripple and tattoo our lungs and our souls as Chinese and Indians do their feet and their skins. We must not pamper the pride and vanity that consume and curse the needful avarice that *honestly* pays the bills. For this is not fair. When we would see social and civil evils, we must not look with fools' eyes to the ends of the earth; to Rome, or Hindoostan, or China, or Japan, but to our own country, our own altars, our own hearts and homes, and looking rightbly with our *candle in hand*, we shall see much indeed to commend, but not a little to censure and reform, for *true manhood*, the basis of all other good, is a *rare and a high endowment*, and we should ever be on our guard against being baffled and deceived by its mere specious semblances and pretences.

Our existing educational forms and systems, in the family, the school, the church and the state, have done tolerably well, but they have outlived their day. They never really and heartily aimed to produce *true manhood* but merely to engender intelligence, taste, scholarship, respectability, to refine and adorn its modes of manifestation. They were made to be, and have become the willing instruments of cast and form. "Jeshurun has waxed fat and kicked. He hath forsaken *God* that made him, and lightly esteemed the rock of his salvation." The bone and muscle of our revolutionary times is giving place to obesity and drowsiness; the effeminacy and appoplexy of the dead and buried nations that have gone before us.

New lands may save us for a time, but *new souls* would do it far better and far longer.

"Marvel not that I say unto you, ye MUST be born again." We do not now mainly need more means, more refinements, respectabilities and forms; more sciences evolving the powers of lightning and steam; more intelligences, exploring all heights and all depths; more languages, grammars, rhetorics and literatures, elaborating and refining the harangues of the senate and the church; more philosophers engendering the expediences and sophisms of the schools. "Let not these be thy gods, O, Israel!" But we need more RADICAL, SELF-EVIDENT TRUTHS, setting our real sins in order before our eyes, and calling with *trumpet tongue* for the *justice of Heaven and the freedom of the soul.*

Dispelling and driving before them, like the the chaff *before the whirlwind*, the absurd dogmas of both sects and sceptics and all the little miserable mists and fogs and drizzles of the church; the petty expediences and caucusings and wire-workings and office-seekings, and humble-servantisms and compromisings and Union-savings and agonisms, and all the fog and foam and froth and filthy slime and scum of the State. To give us a *clear sky* and a *fair sea*, with true manhood at our helm, the smile of Heaven's *light*, and the bow of Heaven's *promise* over our heads, and we OURSELVES *willing* to see the *salvation* of *God.* And when such educational means have performed their true work, we *shall*, on earth as in Heaven, have no need of the light of the candle, nor of the light of the sun, nor of the moon, for the Lord God and the lamb shall give us light, and we shall reign for ever more. So mote it be.

Young gentlemen of the Platonian Society, you have a great work on hand. Your education and position in human society, imposes on you, preeminently, the task, first, of BEING, and second of MAKING MEN—men for the republic, men for the true church, men for time, men for God and eternity. I promised in the outset that I would not be personal; I will keep my promise, even against my feelings and the interest of my cause, lest too plain speech in presence of noble men should be construed into flattery. But it is your good fortune not to be under the necessity of going a hundred miles from home to find a TRUE MAN, and I trust, several of them, who—some of them, at least—have made themselves such, in spite of all possible outward embarrassments, obstacles and disadvantages. Multitudes you can find everywhere, on the other hand, who, in spite of all possible advantages of wealth, education, scholarship, culture, and social and civil aids, are still only *things—gilded things*, ever on sale; as really two legged, and still, as really featherless and soulless as Plato's poor chicken.

Learn then, from these, and know that it is not in the power of wealth, fortune, fate, culture, education, books, teachers, scholarships, talents, gifts, opportunities, stations, offices, churches, states, empires, men or angels, to put true manhood into you, if you will not have it there; nor will all earth, heaven or hell keep it out, if you truly seek it. For God makes a man of EVERY ONE who wants to be a man, and neither God nor the devil will or can make one of any one else.

First, then, learn to look through all outward shams and semblances and see the true man wherever you meet him.

Second, resolve yourselves, individually, to be THE TRUE MAN.

Third, help God and all the great and good, in the great work of making and perfecting TRUE MEN. This is your life work. This is more and greater than founding empires, states, schools and churches; yea, more, greater and higher than creating new globes and new worlds. The noblest work of God—and God aid and bless you in your effort and your work.

www.ingramcontent.com/pod-product-compliance
Lightning Source LLC
LaVergne TN
LVHW020643110826
845149LV00004B/1334

* 9 7 8 1 4 1 8 1 9 0 5 2 1 *